Making Pot

John Anderson

Smith
Settle

First published in 1998 by
Smith Settle Ltd
Ilkley Road
Otley
West Yorkshire
LS21 3JP

ISBN 1 85825 093 5

British Library Cataloguing-in-Publication data:
A catalogue record for this book is available from the British Library.

Set in Monotype Plantin

Designed, printed and bound by
SMITH SETTLE
Ilkley Road, Otley, West Yorkshire LS21 3JP

Introduction

This book is concerned with traditional techniques as practised in an almost vanished type of workshop sometimes referred to as a 'country pottery'. It is based on a specific potter, Isaac Button of Soil Hill Pottery at Causewayfoot, north of Halifax. In all basic respects Soil Hill was typical of the several potteries formerly working in that area, and indeed of those in other districts too. Pots for farm and kitchen use were made in red earthenware: bread crocks, casseroles, chicken-feeders, dog bowls, flowerpots, mixing bowls, storage jars. Tableware was made at a pottery at Denholme, quite near Soil Hill. It closed before 1914, but in the mid-1960s older people in the area still remembered 'Denholme China'.

Until the 1930s such potteries might be found in any district where there was a demand, where there was suitable clay, and where fuel — wood or coal — could be had at a reasonable price. Direction of labour during the Second World War war probably precipitated the extinction of some, and very few survived beyond the 1960s. The obvious cause for decline was the decreasing demand for traditional earthenware pots for kitchen, farm and horticultural use, in the face of competition from cheaper and lighter plastic equivalents. Another factor was that a country potter's sons might well see the family business as a less attractive prospect than alternative employment in the neighbourhood.

There had been potteries in the area between Halifax, Bradford and Keighley before 1650. Soil Hill Pottery was set up in 1780 by Jonathan Catherall, who had come from Flintshire about ten years earlier and started a pottery at Keelham, about a mile (1.5km) east of Soil Hill. Members of the Catherall family worked Soil Hill until 1880. While different sources give slightly different dates, Isaac Button stated that his grandfather, also Isaac Button, had established himself on the site in 1884.

Certainly Grandfather Isaac Button had made a study of good pottery practice and about 1890 rebuilt the premises — using bricks made on site. The layout of the buildings was such as to minimise distances clay, pots and coal had to be carried; hot flue gases from the down-draught kiln, the first of its type in the area, were led under the clay-drying gallery to hasten the process. I assume that a Lancashire boiler installed in the drying room, stoked from the kiln shed, dated from this time; it had powered a steam engine which drove the potters' wheels, blunger, pug mill and other machinery until electric power came about 1946. Grandson Isaac Button joined the business in 1916 at the age of thirteen. For a time in the early 1930s he worked in other potteries, but by 1939 he was one of thirteen working at Soil Hill. His father died in 1943 and he, in partnership with his brother, took over. The brother withdrew in 1954 and for ten years Isaac worked the pottery single-handed.

When he retired in 1964 he moved to South Devon, but the climate proved too soft for his liking, and before long he was back, only a stone's throw from Soil Hill. He died, aged only sixty-six, in 1969. A typical Yorkshireman, Isaac Button was perhaps not a man to bear fools gladly. But for anyone with a serious interest in the work he was doing, nothing was too much trouble.

Though for long largely abandoned in industrial production, the traditional hand-throwing technique survives — if rarely with comparable skill — in many small craft or 'studio' potteries. Many of these concentrate on decorative pieces perhaps for a local tourist trade, but some, including artists of international renown for their 'one-off' decorative work, also make tableware and other useful pieces. Such wares, more usually stoneware or porcelain than earthenware, are every bit as fit for their purpose as are their industrial counterparts, and their individuality gives great pleasure in use.

Acknowledgements

The author gratefully acknowledges his long association with Sheila and Robert Fournier, craft potters and teachers. Without their teaching, albeit informal, he could never have contemplated compiling this book.

Apart from the illustration on page 6, all the photographs in this book are by the author, and were taken between 1961 and 1964. Some are frame-enlargements from a film, *Isaac Button — Country Potter*, directed by Robert Fournier, and photographed and edited by the author.

Isaac Button (extreme left) with fellow workers at another pottery in the Halifax area, about 1930. The pots, seen here drying, are very similar to those made at Soil Hill. Red-firing earthenware clay has been exploited at a number of sites on the west-facing slopes near the present A629 Keighley to Halifax road.

Soil Hill Pottery from the south-west, in 1964. The potters' wheels were situated in a room at the far end of the building. The long drying room *(see pages 28 & 29)* came next, then the kiln room, with the large sliding steel door (and sagging roof ridge). The stock room *(see pages 44 and 45)*, with two small windows, was at the near end, complete with loading platform inside the big sliding wooden door — where an old (1926) lorry was kept. For long unroadworthy, this was used until about 1960 for transporting clay on site.

Clay Preparation. The base of the chimney, seen at top right, helps to relate this photograph to that on the previous page. The clay-drying gallery, under the corrugated iron roof on the right, was along the north wall of the drying room. Three types of clay were available at Soil Hill: the red-firing earthenware clay used for making the pots; a clay which fired a slightly creamy white, used for slip, the light-coloured clay applied to some pots; and a fireclay used to make kiln shelves. In 1963-64, red clay was being taken from just below the topsoil in a shallow pit next to the pottery buildings. Usually, freshly-dug clay was left to weather for some months or even a year or more. A pile of weathered clay can be seen on the left, ready to be mixed with water in the blunger *(seen in more detail opposite)* to form a liquid slip. The slip was run through a sieve suspended from the chains *(see also overleaf)* and via a wooden trough (seen here leaning beside the door) into the clay-drying gallery, under the corrugated iron roof.

The sieve receiving slip from the blunger. As the sieve was swung on its chains, at the end of each swing towards the potter it hit a stop. This jerked the pebbles and coarse grit strained out along to that end of the sieve, where they fell out clear of the slip trough.

The Clay-Drying Gallery. Flues from the kiln passed under these flags — rather like a Roman hypocaust. Over several days, surplus water evaporated from the slip, leaving suitably plastic clay. From here the clay was taken by wheelbarrow through the door *(page 8)* to the pug mill *(see overleaf)*.

The Pug Mill.
Rather like a big mincing machine, this ensures the clay is thoroughly mixed and gets rid of any air pockets. A pile of clay from the drying gallery can be seen in the background. This would be pugged and left to sour for a month or two; then, as shown here, re-pugged not long before use.

The wing of the building housing the pug mill also served as a clay store, and was adjacent to the throwing room where the pots were made.

Weighing Clay. All the pots made at Soil Hill were hand-thrown on the wheel. Balls of clay of the correct size for the pots to be made were weighed out and stacked conveniently to the wheel. For larger pots such as cider jars (taking 28lb/12.5kg of clay), a smaller ball was taken off the main lump, flung down on the wheel-head first and smoothed to a slightly conical shape. This helped ensure that no air was trapped when the main ball was thrown down. The photographs on the following pages give some idea of the different stages and actions of throwing, but can give little hint of the speed and economy of movement of a really skilled repetition thrower. In his prime, Isaac Button could throw a ton (1,000kg) of clay into pots in a day; in 1964 the author filmed him throwing dog bowls — about 1lb (500g) of clay. At first they were being lifted from the wheel every twenty-two seconds, but he finished a run of 200 in an hour.

Throwing a Plant Pot. A ball of clay, previously weighed out, was flung down on the rotating wheel-head (not shown). In stages 1 and 2, the clay is being centred on the wheel. In 3 and 4 it is opened out, forming a ring of clay and defining the bottom of the pot. In stage 5 the hole in the bottom can be seen, and the clay is about to be pulled up to form a cylinder, as in 6 and 7. The process so far is much the same for almost any final form, but here the thick rim of the finished pot has already begun to appear. From stage 8 onwards, the plant-pot form emerges; the cylindrical form is pulled to the full

height of the final pot — as shown by the gauge-stick — before the conical or tapered shape is given. In stages 9, 10 and 11, a steel blade — made from a piece of an old spade — is used in shaping the outside of the pot. It removed most of the conspicuous throwing marks. In stage 12, the wheel has been allowed to slow down and the pot has been cut from the wheel-head using a loop of wire. The name of the potter and the pottery are imprinted using a roulette and the pot is lifted off on to a board, to be carried away to dry. The complete process took about a minute and a quarter.

In good weather, the boards of freshly-thrown pots might be taken outside to dry. In poor weather the drying room was available *(pages 28 and 29)*; this could be heated by the boiler.

(Top) Outdoors, sun and wind would speed drying, but unless the pots were turned at intervals the effect would be uneven, leading to distortion and perhaps cracking. *(Right)* These large pots were the only items at Soil Hill to be marked with the roulette.

Throwing a Stew Pot. In stage 1 the clay has been centred and pulled up to form a cylinder. There is already a flare at the lip where the flange supporting the lid will be formed, a process commencing in stage 2.

By stage 3 the pot nears its final form and further attention is being given to the flange. As with the plant pot, a steel blade or 'rib' was used to remove most of the throwing marks; this has been done in stage 4. Lifted from the wheel, the pots were left to become 'leather hard' before the handles were put on.

I

Handling a Stew Pot.
Sausages of very soft clay
were formed between the
palms of the hands (1);
pressed firmly on to the
leather-hard stew pot in
the required position (2);
smoothed with the thumb
and forefinger (3);
and the ends made
neat, to give the
finished handle (4).

2

3

4

Throwing a Cider Jar. In stage 1, the first pull up towards a cylinder is shown; for a pot as tall as this, the potter needs to stand. In stage 2 the distinctive shape begins to appear; in stage 3 *(opposite)* the narrow neck begins to be formed.

'A Job Well Done.' A favourite moment in the film *Isaac Button — Country Potter*; the finished cider jar is about to be lifted from the wheel. With pots of this size — by no means the largest he made — he used a cow's rib across his forearms in lifting the pot from the wheel. The mark this has left can be seen on the finished pot, opposite.

Slipping a Mixing Bowl.
When 'leather-hard', mixing bowls were 'slipped' on the inside surface — coated with a light-coloured clay. Sufficient slip for several bowls was poured from a bucket into the first bowl, swirled around to cover the entire inside evenly and the surplus poured into the next bowl. A small surplus from the last bowl went back into the bucket.

A board of five slipped mixing bowls, carried outside to finish drying. As mentioned earlier, pots drying outdoors needed turning from time to time to prevent uneven drying.

The Drying Room. Racks in the drying room accommodated the boards on which completed pots, such as these bread crocks, were placed.

When much harder — but still not bone dry — pots could be stacked, base to base and lip to lip, like the bread crocks, slipped mixing bowls and plant pots seen here.

Glazing. At Soil Hill, pots were raw-glazed; the glaze was applied to the unfired pots, which then needed firing once only. Traditional lead glazes were used, consisting of a lead compound, flint dust and clay, all finely ground and suspended in water. In the kiln these materials combined to form the shiny glaze which, chemically, is a type of glass.

The glaze on the insides of pots at Soil Hill contained lead in the form of red lead oxide (lead sesquioxide); that on the outside, galena, one of the principal lead ores — a naturally occurring lead sulphide. Isaac Button was allowed by the Factory Inspectorate to use these glazes only because he had no employees — their toxicity, especially that of the red lead glaze, presents a hazard to the potter. If properly made and fired, there is no danger to the user; but lead-glazed ware from some country potteries has been found wanting.

A cupful of glaze was poured round the inside of a bread crock, swirled around to cover all round, and the surplus poured back into the bucket. The outside was glazed by dipping. Both glazes needed constant stirring to keep the materials in suspension. Finally, the flange or rim where the lid rests was wiped clear of glaze — lids were fired *in situ* and any glaze there would stick the lid immovably in position!

Packing the Kiln. Above, a general view in the kiln shed. One of six firemouths can be seen on the right; above it, blocked by a brick, a spyhole. On the right, inside the partly-packed kiln. The shelves, made of fireclay, weighed about 8olb (36kg); before each was lifted into position, it was carefully inspected and any fragments of glaze from the previous firing chipped off. The majority of the pots made at Soil Hill were not glazed outside at the bottom and could therefore be fired standing directly on the shelves — or on circular batts standing on wads or bobs of fireclay on top of other pots *(see overleaf)*.

Top: wads of fireclay placed round the rim of a pot. *Right:* a circular batt rests on the wads and supports another pot.

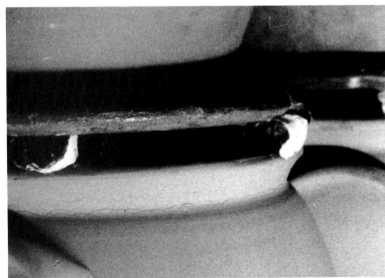

A 'bung' of mixing bowls in the kiln. The underside of the rim was not glazed, and so could safely rest on the flanges of the four curved supports. Plant pots can be seen to the left, stacked one inside the other.

hen the kiln was filled, the doorway
as bricked up and 'clammed' —
lastered over with waste clay.

Towards the end of a working day,
ie fires were lit and allowed to burn
owly overnight. Although apparently
one-dry when put into the kiln, some
ee water was still present, and this
ow heating to 200°C or more
vaporated it.

In the morning the firing began in
arnest as the draught was allowed to
ke hold and a deep, hungry roar
ame from the six firemouths. They

needed stoking every
thirty minutes or so
for the next forty-
eight hours, burning
two and a half tons
(2,500kg) of best coal.

To have worked Soil
Hill single-handed for
ten years is impressive;
to have fired single-
handed every three
months is Herculean.

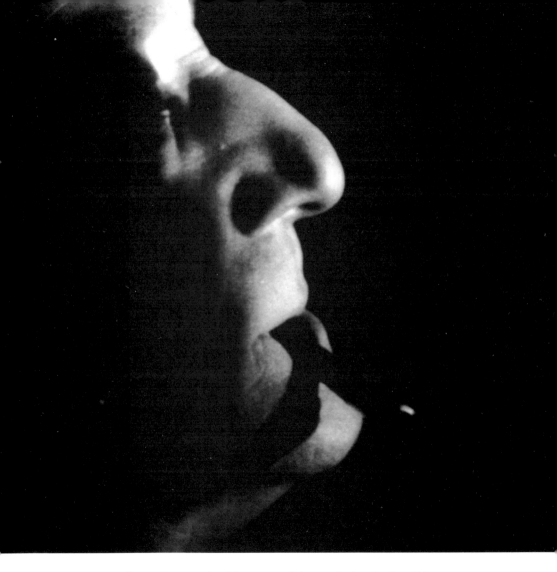

Isaac Button checking one of the spyholes during firing.

The silent witness: a pyrometric cone in the cold kiln confirming that firing has been correct; the tip has bent over so it is level with the base of the cone. Three ways of judging the progress of firing were used at Soil Hill. A thermo-electric pyrometer gave a measure of temperature at one point in the kiln. There were spyholes through which pyrometric cones could be observed. And at the very top of the kiln, test rings were placed. When the pyrometer showed that 1,080°C had been reached and when the cones had gone down, the final check was to clamber over the roof of the kiln shed to the very summit of the kiln, to slide a slab away from the twenty inch (50cm) diameter opening — clearly visible on page 33 — and from the blinding incandescence of the firing, hook out a test ring to check that the glaze had matured adequately. If all was well, the firemouths were clammed up and the kiln left to cool.

One of the Last Firings at Soil Hill. Two or three days later, the moment of truth. The kiln doorway has been broken open and tidied up, and three months' work revealed. It was usually magnificent, with only a tiny sprinkling of failures.

Bread crocks, a casserole and storage jars can be seen on the highest visible shelf. Unlike the majority of Soil Hill ware, the jugs on the next shelf had to be fired on stilts to prevent the glaze, which extends over the foot, sticking to the shelf. Beside the dog bowls on the third shelf down can be seen the pyrometric cone.

The still-warm pots, glaze sparkling, were lifted out.

A completed bread crock. Notice the unglazed lid; this was turned knob inwards so that pots could be stacked in the later stages of drying, and for firing.

Some pots might be stacked by the kiln room door ready for collection by customers.

Most pots would be taken to the adjacent stock room

nixing bowls and plant pots by the dozen.

Isaac Button with the 'dry pan' at Soil Hill. Though disused for some time by the 1960s, its function had been to pulverise fireclay before use.

For some years after Isaac Button's retirement, refractory crucibles for glass manufactur were built at the pottery. During this period, the buildings were allowed to deteriorate badl and the kiln was virtually wrecked by over-firing. Proposals have been made to restore th site as a working museum, but its future is very uncertain. Meanwhile, Isaac Button' skills survive in some measure on film, as an inspiration to present-day craftsmer